LITTLE LIBRARY

In Egyptian Times

Christopher Maynard

Kingfisher Books

Contents

Long, long ago

A great many years ago, the Ancient Egyptians lived in splendour beside the Nile River. Nearly 5,000 years have passed since they started building their lands into a rich and powerful empire, which lasted for 3,000 years.

Land of the Nile

K emi means Black Land, and it was what the Egyptians called their country. The name came from the rich black soil in which farmers grew their crops. To either side of Kemi lay dry dusty desert – the Red Land.

It is very hot in Egypt and it hardly ever rains, so water for crops came from the Nile. The best farming land was in Lower Egypt, where the Nile splits into lots of little rivers before reaching the Mediterranean Sea.

Every summer, heavy rains and melting snow in countries to the south of Egypt made the Nile River flood.

The flood waters dropped rich black mud on the land. Farmers needed the water and mud to grow new crops.

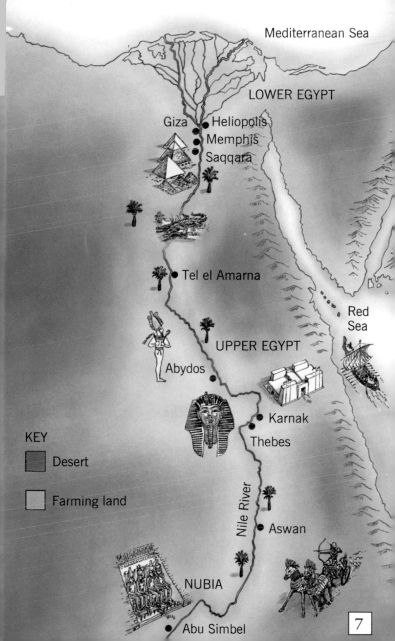

Mediterranean Sea

LOWER EGYPT

Giza • Heliopolis
• Memphis
• Saqqara

• Tel el Amarna

Red
Sea

UPPER EGYPT

Abydos

• Karnak
Thebes

KEY

Desert

Farming land

Nile River

• Aswan

NUBIA

• Abu Simbel

7

Farming the land

Farmers ploughed and sowed their fields in October, as soon as the floods went down. Their main grain crops were wheat and barley, which they used to make bread. Barley was also made into beer.

Fields were small, with narrow canals running around them bringing water from the Nile.

⑥

③

HARVESTING THE GRAIN CROP

① In March or April, the crop was measured by government officials, who worked out how much had to be paid in taxes.

② The ripe ears were cut from the stalks.

③ At the threshing floor, oxen trod the ears to separate the grain from the straw.

④ The grain was tossed, to let the wind blow away the chaff (the outer cover).

⑤ Officials counted and wrote down how many baskets of grain were gathered.

⑥ The grain was stored in granaries.

Living in a town

Almost all Egyptians lived in towns or villages, in houses built from dried mud-bricks. Thick walls helped to keep houses cool inside, while high windows let in air and light.

Roofs were the best places to catch a cool breeze. People often worked up there. Some wove cloth, others made baskets, or worked with wood.

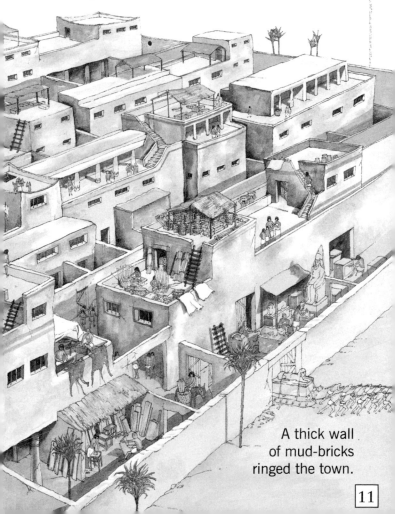

A thick wall of mud-bricks ringed the town.

Food and cooking

Most people lived on beans, bread, onions and beer. Sometimes they ate fish, but meat was rare. Rich people ate all sorts of fruit and vegetables, and lots of geese and duck, too.

Ordinary people had really simple kitchens. Bread was baked in a mud-brick oven.

There were big stones for grinding flour, and a few clay bowls and cooking pots.

DESERT DESSERT

The delicious fruit of the date palm ripens in August. It was eaten fresh, or dried in the Sun so that it could be stored. The Egyptians loved sweet things, and this recipe must have been very popular. You will need:

225 g dates
1 tsp cinnamon
$\frac{1}{2}$ tsp cardamom
100 g walnuts
Honey
100 g ground
  almonds

1 Ask a grown-up to help you blend the dates into a paste with a little water.
2 Chop the walnuts. Add the walnuts and spices to the paste.

3 Mix everything well, then shape the paste into lots of little balls.
4 Dip the balls into the honey, then the almonds – delicious!

An Egyptian villa

Nearly all good land was used for farming in Ancient Egypt, so only rich people could afford to build large houses with gardens.

DRESSING UP

Styles changed, but rich people dressed like this about 3,000 years ago. Clothes were made from pleated linen.

KEY TO THE HOUSE

① Main doorway into the house
② Roof terrace
③ Pool and garden
④ Homes of servants and farm workers
⑤ Stables
⑥ Store rooms
⑦ Animal pens
⑧ Granaries, for storing grain
⑨ Well for water

15

Going to school

Girls stayed home in Egypt, where they were taught weaving and other skills by their mothers. Schools were mostly for boys from wealthy families. The schools were next to the temples, and the teachers were priests. They were strict – any lazy pupil was sure to be punished with a beating.

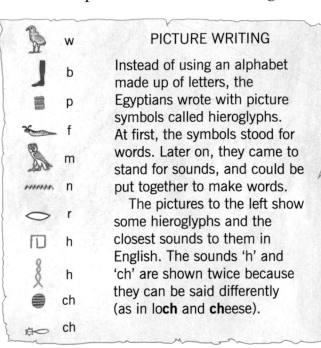

🦅	w
🦵	b
▦	p
🐛	f
🦉	m
〰〰	n
⬯	r
🔲	h
🧬	h
⬤	ch
⚔	ch

PICTURE WRITING

Instead of using an alphabet made up of letters, the Egyptians wrote with picture symbols called hieroglyphs. At first, the symbols stood for words. Later on, they came to stand for sounds, and could be put together to make words.

The pictures to the left show some hieroglyphs and the closest sounds to them in English. The sounds 'h' and 'ch' are shown twice because they can be said differently (as in lo**ch** and **ch**eese).

Boys sat cross-legged on the ground and were taught in groups. They had to learn a lot of things off by heart, and they learned to read hieroglyphs by chanting long lists of them out loud every day.

Students practised their writing using reed brushes on pieces of stone or broken clay pots. Later on they were allowed to write on a type of paper called papyrus, which was made from river reeds.

Trading expeditions

The Egyptians traded with their neighbours for things they could not grow or make themselves.

Egypt had few trees, so ships were sent north to Lebanon for cedar wood. Traders also brought back silver and slaves. In Nubia, the Egyptians traded for gold and copper. They went south to Central Africa and returned with ivory, ebony wood and ostrich plumes.

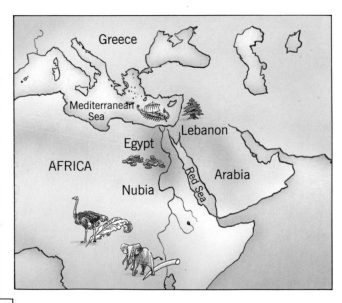

Egyptian traders went to Punt for sweet-smelling incense. No one now knows exactly where Punt was, but historians think it was either in East Africa or across the Red Sea.

A famous expedition to Punt is recorded in an Egyptian temple's wall-carvings. The traders brought incense trees back in special baskets and replanted them in the temple gardens.

The pharaoh's palace

The king of Egypt was called the pharaoh, and he was the most important person in the whole country. He owned all the land and all the people. The pharaoh was a living god, too – the Egyptians believed that he was the son of their Sun god, Ra.

The pharaoh wore a crown and a false beard for special ceremonies.

The pharaoh and the queen sat on thrones in the Great Hall. Servants fanned them with ostrich plumes.

The pharaoh lived in a beautiful palace, surrounded by his family, noble lords and ladies, and a vast army of officials and servants. The Great Hall was the place where the pharaoh carried out government business and listened to his people's problems and quarrels. He could settle them on the spot, for he was also the highest judge in the land.

Going to war

The pharaoh was head of the army and he led his soldiers into battle. Most Egyptians went to war on foot, but the nobles fought from war chariots. Weapons included daggers, spears, axes and bows and arrows.

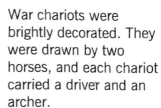

War chariots were brightly decorated. They were drawn by two horses, and each chariot carried a driver and an archer.

After the Egyptians conquered Nubia to the south, they built a chain of great forts to guard their new lands.

MAKE A DAGGER

You'll need some thick card, a pencil, scissors and some bronze paint.

Copy the outline of this dagger on the card. Cut it out and paint both sides.

Temples and gods

Temples were the homes of the gods, and because they were such important places they were built from great blocks of stone. Many are still standing in Egypt today. The largest and wealthiest temple was that of the god Amun at Karnak. This picture shows part of it – the hypostyle hall.

Scenes from battles were carved on the outside of the temple walls.

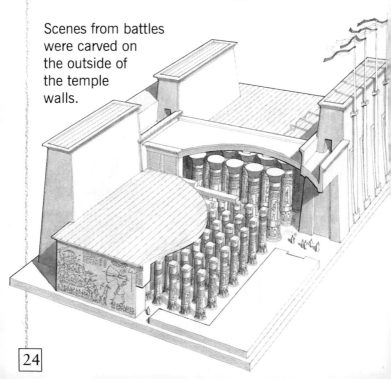

GODS AND GODDESSES

These are just some of the hundreds of Egyptian gods and goddesses. Many were connected with animals.

Amun created the world and looked after Egypt.

Anubis, god of the dead, had the head of a jackal.

Hathor, goddess of love, had cow's horns on her head.

Horus, the sky god, had a falcon's body.

Isis was goddess of Egyptian women.

Khnum made babies on his potter's wheel. He had a ram's head.

Maat was goddess of truth.

Osiris was god of death and rebirth.

Ra was the god of the Sun.

Sebek was the crocodile-headed god of water.

Anubis   Osiris   Horus

Life after death

The Egyptians believed that the dead went to live in a world much like this one, where they still needed their bodies. Because of this, people took trouble to make sure that dead bodies didn't rot away. They learned how to keep bodies, as mummies.

A salty mixture was packed over the body to dry and preserve it. Then it was washed, and bandaged up with sweet-smelling spices.

BAKE AN AMULET

Egyptians wore small good-luck charms called amulets. These were wrapped up with mummies, too. As well as a bowl, a rolling pin, plastic film, a baking tray, some poster paints and clear varnish, you'll need:

100 g plain flour
100 g salt
1 tsp oil
60 ml water

1 Mix together the flour, salt, oil and water and knead the dough until it is smooth and stretchy.
2 Wrap it in plastic film and chill it in the fridge for 24 hours.

4 Turn the shape on to a greased baking tray and peel off the plastic film.
5 Ask a grown-up to bake it for you, at gas mark 4 (180°C), for 15 minutes.
6 Seal your amulet with varnish when cool. Thread a ribbon through it and hang it round your neck.

3 Roll it out flat on more film, to about 1 cm thick. Cut out the amulet shape shown right.

The pyramids

After a pharaoh died, his body was carefully preserved as a mummy. Until about 3,500 years ago, all the pharaohs' mummies were buried in gigantic stone tombs called pyramids. In later years, they were placed in tombs cut deep into rock cliffs.

The pyramids were so well built that many are still standing to this day. The biggest one of all, the Great Pyramid at Giza, took more than 30 years to build, using over 2.3 million huge stone blocks.

INSIDE THE GREAT PYRAMID

The burial chambers for the pharaoh and his queen were filled with all the things they would need to make them comfortable in the afterlife – from beds, tables and chairs, to clothes and food.

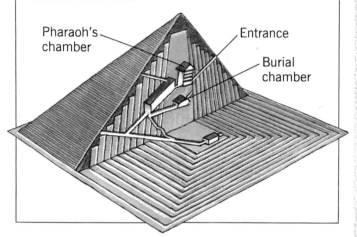

Pharaoh's chamber

Entrance

Burial chamber

No one knows exactly how the pyramids were built. Each stone block weighed more than two cars do today, and was very difficult to move.

Blocks were probably slid along on wooden sledges or rollers.

Index